THOSE WHO ARE LEFT BEHIND

Sabina Asar-Browne

MINERVA PRESS

LONDON
ATLANTA MONTREUX SYDNEY

THOSE WHO ARE LEFT BEHIND
Copyright © Sabina Asar-Browne 1998

ISBN 0 75410 272 6

First Published 1998 by
MINERVA PRESS
195 Knightsbridge
London SW7 1RE

Printed in Great Britain for Minerva Press

THOSE WHO ARE LEFT BEHIND

To the late Diana, Princess of Wales. Compassion is like a work of art putting into words that which comes purely from the heart.
Mankind experiences its own cortège of feelings each ticking second of the day, but like the floral tribute the stem of each flower gives us the hope to carry on.

I felt I knew you,
Hence I mourn you more
Than you ever know.
I mourn a million hearts,
I mourn many thoughts,
I think for the grieved,
I recall many a loss.

Acknowledgements

I would like to thank Eugene for his encouragement, and my children Maurice, Diana and Daniel who could foresee this book becoming a reality.

I would also like to thank Minerva Press for making the publication of *Those Who Are Left Behind* possible.

Preface

Born in Ghana in the early Fifties, I was adopted and brought to Britain at the age of nine. My adopted father, an English doctor and surgeon, encouraged me academically by sending me to independent boarding schools in Seaford, Sussex, and Uckfield, Sussex.

I went straight into nursing and midwifery and qualified in 1977. Later I went on to study social work and counselling. I started writing poetry in 1995 and have had a number of poems published by *Poetry Today* (Penhaligon Pages) and *Poetry Now*. I am also a member of the National Society of Poets.

I realised my potential lay with bereavement poetry after my initial poem, 'Feelings', which was published in a Church magazine. I guess I am a deep, spiritual person and hold the belief that there is a more in-depth way of looking at life. With these poems, I aim to deliver hope and tranquillity and, most of all, liberation from fears and uncertainties that are associated with loss and death. I sincerely hope that this collection of poetry will inspire others to be stronger and give them a will to survive.

Those Who Are Left Behind should not surrender their wills to survive but look ahead to a brighter day.

A Floral Tribute

Rest in peace now you have ceased,
Sleep for now till we meet.
Your existence is all that flowers,
And on the petals of each flower
A million tears you will see,
And in each fragrance the flower gives
A million memories in a mind do yield,
And when the leaves on each flower reveal
Its age, its withering, and its sort,
Those that are left are assortments,
Assortments of your compassion, my friend.
Then perhaps the stem on each
Becomes our strength to carry on.

Those Who Are Left Behind

Borrowed for a time, in time
An entry was made for life
for those who are left behind,
That it should show compassion.
And now they'll not borrow,
they refused to stay behind,
And in the minds of those who think
They think the same as others think.

I seek permanence, permanence will do.
I seek answers, questions will not do.
I seek what should not be.
I see the hereafter not in this life.
I seek immortality nothing else.
I seek permanence, I seek immortality.
I seek your life again,
Borrowed for a time only.

An entry was made for life
And now I seek permanence.
A million tears will not do.
A million tributes will not do.
A million verses will not do.
A million words will not do.
Nothing in a million will ever do.

Brighter Days

I sit and think of brighter days, again and again I think,
I rehearse your life and mine, again and again I rehearse.
Will there be brighter days for me?
The seasons come and go, so set me upon a platform of
Audiences and explain the things I long to hear,
Like brighter days, freshness, and cheer,
Like beauty and flowers, and the radiant sun,
Like youth and innocence, side by side,
And when brighter days fill the earth.
Your memories will fill these days.

Compassion

Compassion is like the work of art
Deeply rooted within the heart
Revealing feelings of innermost thoughts.
And it's not because I've been there,
It's not because I understand
Suffering, being there, and understanding
Doesn't make me who I am.
Who I am made me compassionate first.

The Drumbeat

Distant sound you summon me,
In the hallways of mind
I feel your movement upon my ears,
Under the soles of my feet.
I tap and rhyme to your beat.
In my solitude you return to call me.
You perform for me sweet calm,
Racing against my heartbeat.
Within my breast you return
Like peace upon a troubled ocean.

And in the stillness of the night
You journey a thousand miles to
The resting place where I once was born.
You tell them I'm well and not come to harm,
And when you return I've been with you
On your journeys far and wide.

Rhythms of the barrel,
telling stories of footsteps,
marching, calling the great parade,
You make a public spectacle of bravery,
You make martyrs of saints,
You summon missed heartbeats,
You panic man's fear of death.

Feelings

I got the news today
Just as I closed my door.
Like so many times before
That unexpected letter came.
That unexpected letter said
Died in his sleep, I regret.
The twisted writing on the page,
The words which now cause my grief,
In that unexpected letter reads.
You died in your sleep, the letter said.

No words, no pain for the end,
Just that your head had gone to bed,
Then the feelings were back again
So sharp like a daggers edge,
So deep, too deep to see.
What do I feel now you've gone?
No more tables to be laid for two,
No more happy words, or tearful joy,
And those cold winter morns
You would roll up like a ball.

Feelings, just feelings.
I wonder what you must have felt
The moment you went to eternal rest.
I wonder what you must have thought,
As we often ought to pause,
And take account of life's destiny.
Death's cold hand upon your brow
You lie alone and quite unstirred,
No one to share your final hour,
No one to walk that lonely road.

So it is with feelings, feelings;
Feelings of life, feelings of death,
Feelings of loss, feelings of love,
Feelings to live, feelings to be born,
Feelings of your life when you breathed.

Death Unspoken

Along the path of life
Is a place that never speaks.
It lives in the mind of every mortal being,
It hides from everyday life,
And in its shadow lurks
The thoughts on man's fatality.

Death, why do I not speak your name?
I compare you to a forbidden fruit
That is consumed and never spoken of.
Dare I try to comprehend
The meaning behind your purpose,
For you make your home in no man's land,
Be it desert, ocean or sky, man can die on these.
I search for you in the land of the living.
Side by side you dwell with us.

I pursue your stillness on an empty breath,
Void of silence.
I listen to your message in this elegy,
I clutch on to your emptiness as my words
Return within me, O silent death,
And in my heart I dread your thoughts.

The Fugitive

Green leaves, how you lose your greenness.
When I look at you I see your course,
That one day your freshness will die,
Just like a man when his season comes.
And now I call to mind
The seasons of man and of his life.

Your edges are tainted with decay
And very soon you will shrivel to nought.
I want to put you down,
But in wonder I hold on to you,
Very, very soon to take you home
And rest you upon my potted plants,
Or call my son and tell him your wonder,
Of how different and assorted you become

In the different stages of your growth.
Boredom makes me hold you still
And soon if I like I'll cast you down.
You were plucked from nothing
And thus you'll return.
Not remembering from whence you were
You travelled perhaps a thousand miles,
And here you meet your untimely death.
You remind me of the cruelness of death.

In the prime of your life you intrude with death,
You find your way to seize this life
From one not fully grown.

The Poet's Funeral

O pitiful death,
Pitiful death which denies sympathy,
Let me not mourn thee.
Bringing into memory the dancing of spirits,
Tune upon this single note.
Embrace me with raging passion,
The grip of bliss in another world to come.
Linger on verse after verse,
Whisper sweet emptiness upon a sound
Of a host of angels the words on your epitaph.

Vanish not your rhyme on rhyme
Upon an already trodden road.
Should creators be confined to dust,
To be silenced from the work of art?
Moulded words which shape tomorrow
Return to pound within my trembling heart.

Let there be justice, pitiful death.
Connive not with death, dreadful hour.
Fallacy denies poetic justice of its course.
Mimic not David's instrument upon a harp,
A Goliath in the shape of death.
Consume not the breath of life.
Face to face, darkness to darkness,

I hear your voice in death.
Tell me the hour you consumed
The forbidden fruit.
Tell me when death's cold hand
Reached for your willing eyes,
You bring your charm to haunt us here
As we tread this muddy ground.
Vivid thoughts from pens I recall,
Coloured by the illusions of life.

The Cremation

Promptly you bid me farewell
Amongst the emptiness.
Soon, soon, your fate returns.
Remember me no more as man
But dust to which you must return,
And soon, soon your life read
As you journey into hollowness.
Spectator of a walking shadow,
What mortal doesn't in his mind
Seek to live on borrowed time?
What man receives death with a sword?
What man embraces it with a kiss?
Soon the earth will refuse you home
And soon you'll cease to have been.
Soon your birth will end in soil.

Amidst the confusion of emotion,
Because death was to mask the life
That was, in disguise death did end,
Shock mistakes my presence
In this empty church, void of chorus,
Of sweet melodies.
In my mind's eye I see you pass,
I see you in the row behind.
My eyes follow on along this aisle
Where you and I talked before.

You remain a total stranger
Now your breath has ceased.
No longer part of my circle,
I must lay you to rest.
Now I'll put my grief aside,
At least for this solemn time.
You had always said that if ever
You should die,
That nature was not to be disturbed –
No flowers, no wreaths, no elegy,
No burial in the earth, no tears.
Now you leave my tears to choke within.
What a burden you leave for me.

You summon yourself to hell on earth
Within the oven of a witness,
The evidence that man is only dust
And that one day all must return to it.

I never knew you at all like now
As I take a final look once more.
What helpless mortals, who all too vainly
Refuse and deny mortality.
Life is a theatre of mine
Upon a stage of confused participants.
The curtains now draw back
As you slide into nothingness.

The Noise of a Minute's Silence

Silence, in your hush I can hear your voice,
Can hear in you the voices of the past.
All within my mind is the cheer,
Footsteps and clutter,
Can hear you with my eyes closed,
Can hear you when I am listening.

Can I compare you to a forgotten voice?
In your serenity I hold a conversation
When my mind returns within me.
You respond to me, silence,
And your echoes linger within my mind.
And in a moment you sham my senses.
When I reach out you are not there,
You play hide and seek with my emotions,
You return when my tongue is still.

A Haunting Melody

Verse after verse after verse
Returns to possess me like a haunting.
Leave me to repent in dust,
As the chorus repeats to pound my mind
Of the many times of my denial.

Sweet melodies in muffled sounds,
Out of tune they may seem
To those out of place like me.
Remind me of the many times
To church I've not returned.

I observe my wake as the psalm is read.
O universal death,
In dust shall man end all his days,
And his remnants shall not be his.
O universal life,
I chase an impossible dream,
My joys of motherhood are a token,
My grief in death is the shadow of the past.

The Poet's Love-Song

Deepening love within my bosom,
Mind enchanted with memories
Like magic in urgency,
I seek your face in thoughts.
Miles apart love is never lost.
Conjure images of sweet embrace
That kiss my soul,
Conjure the fragrance of summer nights
That linger on,
Conjure repeated words, like verses
Upon a rhyme,
Then my love will remember.

Then my love will remember.
In my psyche you will remain
Like an obsession between two heart beats.
You take me to that unspoken
Secret between two lovers,
That unspoken magic which binds
The heart of deep love in love.
Kiss, my soul, sweet melodies.
Bring unto memory sweet passion
Like red or white petal flower.
Forced upon a single rose.

Tucked within a soft circle, two by two,
Conjure the fragrance of love.
Along my finger tips I feel your love
And in my memory you will remain.
The passion of sweet love,
Wrapped in one in my psyche will remain.

Life's Lonely Road

There is a quite place in my mind,
A place that only I can go,
And in that tiny place I recall
All that is tranquillity.
It is just a place for thoughts
Of life, of death and of destiny,
And in those thoughts are memories,
Mysteries of memories I have stored.

And like the mirrors of life's distortion
Its reflections are rehearsed,
Rehearsed a thousand times.
Like the wind its whispers are within
But yet as clear as the skies
Are the paths that have seen so many bends.

Now you lie there all alone.
I want my thoughts to journey a while,
I want my thoughts to stop once more.
And if I could journey your thoughts
I would take your lonely life's account
Because in your mind I would ask
Where are those unspoken words you utter,
Not to be heard now your tongue is still

Those words stolen never to be heard,
The thoughts behind those clammy brows,
The tongue within you as still as night
As you lie there quite unstirred.
Will it only be in dreams I can hope?
Where is your life which used to be?
In my loneliness when evening is come,
When night is still and all is peace,
In my search for you I'll never cease
And for me the questions of life
Will begin again – life, where art thou?
Remind me of breath again

So tell me before I'm born
And the questions begin.
A time like this will come upon
Each mortal being that is destined to live:
A time for sorrow, a time for discontent,
A time of pain, a time for grief,
A time for questions, a time of fear,
A time of guilt, a time for a tear,
A time for collecting, a time for dispersing.
Tell me before I am born
That life's a lonely road lived in the mind.
Then if I had a choice
It would have to be not to have been,
Not to have trodden on life's lonely road.

The Mist

Send me no flowers,
Send me no tears,
Spare me those empty words,
Prepared word for word.
Mist is all I see, in my mind,
In my thoughts, in my sleep.
Mist has clouded my happiness,
Like milk in clear water.

Perplexity jumbles my senses.
Like a fugitive I am in exile,
My senses no longer mine.
I feel what I hear,
Feel what I see,
And in my mortal being
Bargain for immortality.
Suddenly the mist begins to form.

August

August, season of rapture,
You rob me of my laughter,
You take away my anniversary
And wedding bells.
You beckon me to the burial ground
And recreate the horror of life.

You bring into recollection
What I choose to disremember,
You make me a bride without a groom,
My flowers do not bring joy but gloom.
You feign my reality when I utter
Into silenceness, my witnesses do not converse

Amidst the confusion of emotion,
That death was to mask the life that was,
Shock mistakes my presence
In this church, void of a chorus,
Of sweet melodies.
In my mind's eye I see you pass,
I see you in the row behind.

And soon, soon your life is read
As a journey into hollowness.
Spectator of a walking shadow,
What mortal does not in his mind
Seek to live on borrowed time?
What man received death with a sword?
What man embraces it with a kiss?
Life is a theatre of a mime
Upon a stage of confused participants.
Now you leave my tears to choke within me,
What a burden you leave for me.

You make me lament in stifling air.
You choke my freshly cut flowers,
You drain me of my tears in a neatly
Folded kerchief.

Death, the Judge

Death, the judge, bringeth execution
At an unappointed time.
Death who holds the key to the grave,
Death the unexpected haste of dust.
I plead for eternity in frail breath
And suddenly I want to live,
I repent of wasted youth.

Suddenly I recall glimpses of fate
In an all forgotten past.
Suddenly life's shadow outreaches
The cold embrace of death.
Smiles and tears exchanged in haste
Confuse my already foggy thoughts,
Death and defeat a monologue in my mind.
Suddenly my senses resurrect within,
And hope cometh at the eleventh.

Nostalgia of my exile days on earth
Bring with hope the way I should live.
Rethinking for me all my lost yesterdays,
Hope thinketh for me the way I should live.
Suddenly I want to live.
I plead for eternity on frail breath.

I repent for wasted youth,
I please for a reprieve
And suddenly I want to live.

The Poet's Delight

Affairs of the heart recalled again
Upon the balance of judgement,
Mind wrestling against the heart,
Solitude offers me an audience
Upon a platform of wishful thoughts.
Thoughts of emptiness of love died,
Bliss of never-ending passion
Cease my mind in the course of thoughts.
Forgetfulness, out of sight for now,
Thrills my every sense.
Aftermath of love revisited,
Hurriedly exploring intense emotions
Upon a soft willing heart,
Take me to the depth of love,
Experience for me feelings of
Butterflies upon an empty stomach.
Where passion sits all alone
Rouse unfeeling senses neglected,
For love anew as dawn breaking
Freshness, unblemished innocence
Recalled into complete rapture.

Love Poem

Take me to the depth of my love
And there you will find
Lurking within this mortal flesh
A wish for permanence,
Of romance sweet, sweet melodies,
Of ballads upon a blissful moment
Uninterrupted by thoughts of hereafter.

In life I seek unity in death
And in death I pursue you still.
A haunting remembrance of attachment
Linger on like fragrance of eternal love.
I search for a token of remembered love
Upon this soft silk cushion,
I lament for no cause but fear.

Come to life O single heartbeat.
Witness for me the breath of love
In a mind twisted with vanity,
And when reality begins to sober
I'll search for that mystery of life,
The mystery that it is better to have
Loved and lost than never to have loved.

Autumn Leaves

In the heap you lay before my feet
You witness the seasons come and go.
Like man you form assortments of life,
Young and old you mix alike.
Should I dare to hope
That in your face life has a beginning,
As you lay across the ground?
Some of you will run a race
To be brought together when the collecting starts.
Just like the trees that stand bare
In this lonely cemetery here you lie.
Void of the soil that gave it life
You take your lead and I'll stay behind,
And when the gathering has began
In the heap I'll find you again.
So as they put you here to rest
I think again of the year ahead.
They tell me in the cards they've sent
That in the days ahead I'll mend,
That surely again the sun will shine,
For you have gone to God divine.

Motherhood

God bless that womb that bore,
The hands that care,
The tears that share the sorrows,
The heart that bears the burden,
The mind that is never resting,
The spirit that knows
The nature of her babes.

God bless the bosom that embraces,
The arms that never cease to welcome.
The force that wills to go on,
Even when all is empty
For the sake of mothering,
Everything that is living
Is a gift of undying love.

The nature of life is there for good.
She will never sleep,
She will mourn her child,
She will mourn her husband,
She will never reveal her grief,
She will leave behind her tears.
Her thoughts are there within,
Deep in her heart they are locked within.

God bless the face that is never seen
But in every living thing
Is the shadow of her thoughts.
And when the cord is cut
There is another stage for her,
Growing from day to day.
The stages of a babe,
The only thing that's left behind
Is the navel that unties.

As they grow some will die.
She will never leave their side,
And if she's first to die
She will never take her eternal rest.
She is the face that is never uncovered,
She is the tears that hide within.
For those she will ever love
She is the gift of undying love.

The Outdooring

Dawn breaks and tradition continues.
They ooze in twos and threes
Like three wise kings in pursuit
Of a new child.
White gowns and gold wraps,
Coral beads and precious metals
Fit for a throne,
Fragrances as sweet as nature,
Captured in white kerchiefs
Conjure for me repeated
Scenes of the joys of motherhood.

Then the gathering begins to form.
Eight days ago he joined the world,
Never seen or breathed outdoors.
He must be shown to his kin.
On this very day child
Take the name of your chosen kin.
Hold it bold in righteous embrace.
Long life, prosperity, fertility,
In your name should we expect.
Respect happiness and peace
Until you are returned to dust.

Florist Florence's Funeral

Which flowers would you have picked
To lay upon your marble grave?
Amidst the roses and carnations and daffodils
Death has no colour it may seem.
All the years you must have seen
Flowers of every kind as nature would have it
As you picked and trimmed for a beloved.
At your finger tips you knew the best
Which should be laid upon your sixty years of life
Now that you have gone to rest.
The aura of my senses conjures for me
The odour of your corner shop,
Of leaves and flowers of every kind.

But tomorrow and the next and the next
My eyes will follow as you board my train,
And in the nothingness I'll not see you again.
Like a bird that's lost its nest,
Who will nourish your little shrub
On the hot August days,
As you lie there never to wake?
The wreath is laid upon your door
Amid the confusion of scorched flowers,
No freshly cut flowers today.
Even the rain can't do
What you always did so well.

So is it today you'll lay beside
The green fields and radiant flowers –
Each type you knew so well,
Could tell with your eyes closed –
But for today with life's uncertainties
You are at perfect peace,
At peace with the things you love.
And underneath your wreath it says,
'Nan, Mum, Gran, Aunt RIP.'

The Table

You form the once upon a time
Upon the minds of infants
Within this nursery room,
Moulding adults of tomorrow,
Fairness and sharing
Upon this wooden board.

Upon you unity gathered,
Upon you division dispersed,
Upon you judgement was cast,
Upon you peace discussed,
Upon you wars were planned,
Upon you treaties were broken,
Upon you decisions were affirmed,
Upon you sentence was read,
Upon you betrayal was deliberated.

Universal symbol of togetherness
We sat alike face to face as children do.
In each childhood year we sat alike.
Within this infants class they sit alike.
Toys and books fought for
Fairness taught and shared alike.
More treasured years, will never forget.

Universal symbol of decision making
In adult life we meet again.
Back to back we sit this time,
Our differences make us a mockery,
A betrayal of our younger years.
Face to face we part again.

Unspoken Words

Unspoken words within my mind's eye
Find no release from being.
Thought for thoughts in all that's nought,
Emptiness from images from within,
Form wordless interpretations.
Closeness denied me, grief forbidden.

Words formed yet not spoken
In my sudden melancholy.
How I urge to escape from myself,
Yet, like a sinner in purgatory,
My words refuse to set me free.
Forbidden rules of not what ought say
My words are saved for who or when.

Speechless speech, you deny me
Of my line.
Tongue-tied within a sober mind,
Confused words is all I see.
Within my bosom is all that's sealed,
Words of how I feel, words of how I feel
Softly treading along the forbidden
Rules of what ought I say what ought not.

April

Season of resurrection of the dead,
All mortality is born again.
You lift the curtain of darkness
Upon nature,
You refuse to let me mourn.
Buttercups, daisies, violets
Cradle the grave along the tomb.
Flowers of remembrance,
You take me along your memory lane,
Or forget-me-nots and evergreens,
You prepare for me beaming days ahead,
A prophecy for the Aprils to come.

Freshness, sinless, upright,
Your showers wash my tears.
Down to my feet you cleanse me.
Your meekness inherits the earth,
Your breath gives me peace.
In your face I see hope,
In your face I see beauty,
Colours and youth.
My grief is turned to joy,
April the season of prospect.

Inner Peace

The secret of happiness is really plain.
The inner contentment of your being
Is in a place called your soul.
If you really try, you can find
A resting place for burdens of life.
It is quite simple if your heart's content
With the simple things in life on earth,
Things that are always there
Like the unending love of God, Creator,
And the goodness of Mother Nature,
The sun that visits all life and
The moon and stars that lead the light
Into eternal light.

But those are things which should not deny
The need to praise the God on high.
The unceasing love He shows to mankind
Is not the quakes that tremble the earth,
Is not the fires that scorch the land,
Is not the ruin of nations and kingdoms,
Is not the wars that cause the drought,
Is not the evil that mankind prefers.
The God of nature is nature itself,

And when nature is at peace
Is the miracle of birth,
And the gift of motherhood,
The miracle of all mankind.
So it is not a lot to ask
To put a little time aside.
Just a time for you and God,
Renewing your soul and giving Him praise,
And His spirit will begin to move.
Then you will discover the secret of inner peace.

In My Tomorrows

And sweet motherhood awaits her still
In the tomorrows of my mind.
In the tears she'll leave behind,
In the shadows of grief untold,
Sweet motherhood will hold her bold.

And sweet motherhood awaits her still
In the tomorrows of my thoughts.
When her child is yet to be born,
In the pains of nature's curse
Sweet motherhood will share her joy.

And sweet motherhood awaits her still
In the tomorrows of my fears.
When her child has yet to walk
Along this journey of life ahead
Sweet motherhood will bear her love.

And sweet motherhood awaits her still
In the tomorrows of my deepest grief.
When she is left to mourn
This barren life that's full of nought
Sweet motherhood will not return.

And when sweet motherhood is laid to rest
In the tomorrow's of my mind,
Amidst the disappointments and delusions
Sweet motherhood will be laid to rest,
Sweet mother will rest at last.

Solemn

Solemn greets like a friend,
For once it greets me a kiss.
A passion for the days to come
It bids me true welcome.
Unrelenting it offers me
Solitude, offers me peace,
And solemn offers me loneliness.

For once loneliness offers me warmth
Void of laughter and cheer.
Temporary solemn offers me indifference
An indifference props me,
Props me when I'm thinking.
Thinking walks with me,
In an unfriendly hour clings with me.

Rainbows

Rainbows, colours of peace.
In death my senses make a scorn
Of my passion.
Colours of a treaty once made.
In death, my death, my senses confuse me
Of your direction.
You form the colours of my mood.
In death my senses choose for me
None of your beauty.
I sort you out to put aside
For another day
What cannot be worn today.

Because today tomorrow can wait.
Like a woman who cannot break her fast,
I long right now for resurrection
Of the one I laid to rest.
My tribulation is more than I can bear
If in a twinkling of an eyelid
Death summons us all.

Rainbow colours that conjure peace.
What might it be if, after the storm,
The leaves remain
Without the tree that nourishes it.
And if at the end of the rainbow
There is no pot of gold, when
Death with its ugly shadow
Images all that life has born.

The Anniversary

Upon an audience of feelings
In turbulent times rescue my thoughts.
Butterflies panic my every sense.
As my heart skips many a beat,
All I feel is panic.
How long has it really been?

Go away, morbid thoughts
Which find no escape from within.
News, I have as much as I hate
The one who brought the news;
News of how it was,
News of how you died,
News of how it felt, news.

O false life lived by lies,
Doubts, but by truth itself.
Evidence is all that's left.
Truth is that you did live,
And how life confuses me still.
Battle continues within a troubled mind,
A haunting is now brought to light.

So, I must make haste once more,
As I've done thrice before,
To that place where mortals lie,
To that unforgotten life that's gone,
Butterflies lingering on
In a heart summoned by love,
And there to place on grass
Picked flowers of interruption.

Brighter Days

I sit and think of brighter days,
Again and again I rehearse your life.
Life has said it all, I guess,
It said it when the curtain fell,
That final curtain which must fall
Upon man's life to be no more.
Then questions and revisions
Are corrections of how life could have been.
Life is no more than a play, it seems
As I rehearse your life again.

You played your part in the play you had,
But in the flashbacks are images,
Rehearsed for whom I do not know.
So set me upon a platform of audiences
And explain the things I long to hear,
Like the thoughts which cannot be felt
And the aches and pains which linger on,

Will there be brighter days for me?
Of normal days when freshness of life,
And greenness of fields cover your face,
Of days when the sun returns to nature
And the snow is shed like tears,
I think of spring and its colours and
I think of when you walked over here.
In every situation I see a scene.
And in these thoughts you witness all these,

And as you lie there all alone
It's shrouded things I conceive.
Then the questions for me begin.
Questions of life and death and destiny,
Questions of where it all must end,
That in a day some life will end,
Sometimes Mum or Dad or kin or friend.
But then I think of brighter days,
Days when you were well and fine,
And somehow the seasons have cheated me
In spring and summer, autumn and winter,
'Cos they will return and will move with time.

Where is the life I used to know
Now the final curtain has fallen?
No need for rehearsals of life's uncertainty.
And like a dark mirror that fails to reflect
I think of your perfect life in mortal thoughts.
(But when I think of brighter days
Brighter days will return won't they?)
Then the memories of your life
Will fill those brighter days.

Vanity

What will you do with your pride
When you are taken from this life?

What will you do with your wealth
When you breathe your final breath?

What will you do with your hate
When death is your only fate?

What will you do with your greed
When there is nothing for you to feed?

What will you do with your lust
When you are returned to the dust?

What will you do with your sloth
When no one can help you out?
What will you do?

Tell Me

Tell me who I was before my birth
Then I might accept death the same.

Tell me life and death were born together
Then I might accept that living is the same.

Tell me that death is peace, absolute peace,
Like the calm of a troubled sea,
Then I won't fight it anymore.
Tell me it's a resting place from life's
Rough roads and its burdens,
Then I won't challenge it when it comes,
When it will be my fault not to be watching.

Grief

I grieve a grief that grieveth me much,
A grief that understandeth me not.
A million flowers I have been,
A million sadnesses I have I felt.
To such that hold dear to me I grieve.

And moments return to flood my thoughts,
Thoughts of man's idle life.
Life snatched from whence it came
And, like a shell that cracks,
Fragments revisit this idle life.

Stormy Love

Love and regrets gather my thoughts
And, one by one, I pick a chance.
A moment revisited holds me to
Memories so dear I can't forget.
Love caresses my tender thoughts
Like blanket over cold embrace.
Love chants for me sweet ballads,
Sting by lovebirds in empty air,
Of warm walks in lovers' lane,
Of passionate kisses in consolation.
United in love the love is one
Between us two. No one knows
Secrets forbidden, purpose known to no one.
Desperate love waits for none but me.
Sweetness with butterness is what we are.
And taught as always before
Unity approved the permissible.

Missed Love

Day after day forms my tomorrows
Of yesterday.
Infatuation begins to possess me
Of the many times your love I'd denied.
Broken dream, hopelessness returns
To claim a prisoned heart.
Like a sentence on broken love
I seek a reprieve.

In the midnight hour I seek reprieve,
And in my solitude I seek reprieve,
That tomorrow in yesterday's dreams
And today be a platform of now,
Devoted time after present,
Tomorrow moves on with the tide.
Interrupt not plans formed today.

I seek the clock which has stopped,
I seek the love which I missed,
I seek you wherever you are.
In my restlessness, I'm not content.

Unhappy Love

Love sparks from nothing,
Bringing momentary solution
Upon a heart void of feeling,
Left empty at length to remember.
Answers return to questions.
Hastily I cling to desire,
Desire of the heart
Confused by the flesh.
Reckon the unreckoning,
Comprehend the uncomprehending.
Passion and rage, an ally of
My true instinct.
Urge and persuasion give in,
And when feeling's separated
Consolation will I not grasp.

Wronged Love

Raging passion returns to possess me
Like wild roses in forgotten garden,
Minds regurgitating upon the flesh,
The forbidden fruit of nature's eyes,
Innocence side by side in paradise.
Linger on thoughts upon thoughts,
Fantasies of the hereafter.
Nurture what nature mocks,
Reality in the midnight hour
Return to day when the bliss,
Of night returns to dawn.

I can hear bitter sweet whispers
Upon unlistening ears and
Unfeeling senses upon the aura
Of your touch.
Purge me in my confusion of moonlight
Kisses and angry words,
And summon for me faithful sleep
Upon my troubled brow.

Moonlight

Love laid beside my lonely heart
Like a beckoning call in the dark
Upon love's mountains of affection,
Luring me to journey the explored
And pounding like bold steps against
My existence, calling for my surrender.

And confusion offers me peace,
In my eleventh hour it gives me choice.
Alien thoughts return to haunt me.
Voices of the past linger on,
But not for now.
Hope glares at me in my mind's eye,
Doubt debates my momentary resolution,
And passion seizes my frantic embrace.

And when my sober senses do return
Passion returns to whence it came,
Leaving the eternal flame of love
Upon bruised love once again.

Emptiness

Weep no more empty tears,
Let yesterday be a haze in life's interruption.
Flow for me the feelings of hope
On eyes free from the cloudiness.
Brighter days lay in wait.
I'll choose sober days to come, as yet
Mourning clothes, out of sight,
As far away to make me forget.

Remember not the tuneless hour
Of sermons and dirges,
Of chorus upon chorus of bleak elegies.
Feel not the stifling air
Of burial grounds and long marches,
Wreaths and flowers, out of sight,
As far away to make me forget.

Remember not the unperfect life
Of the one you've laid to rest,
Of how his life could have been.
Conjure for me the vivid memories
Repeated for me in the well wishes.
Cards and memoirs, out of sight,
As far away to make me forget.

Untitled

Mortal man who feigns life in life
You make death a reason for living.
Scenes of life recited upon
A stage of emptiness, void of darkness
Before the curtain on death is lifted.
Man goes hastily to his grave
Only to be dwelt among for the rest of life.

Nurture with nature, noble man.
On a once upon a time,
Beneath the radiant sun that beams,
Weathered by wind, rain and snow,
Stir for me, O noble breath,
And to life all that's dust.

Colourless death which distorts beauty
Of a clear crystal ball without a future.
There is no hope in tomorrow.
Remove the veil that shadows reality,
Uncover the nakedness of dust
Before the final curtain call.

Consolation

Darkness, hide me under your solace,
Conceal me beneath your veil,
Comfort me within your wings,
Bestow my strength in your frailty.
Let your phantom deny light.
Let your burden travel like
A feather beyond my reason.
Today I bid you friendship

Embrace me in my grief like a cloak.
Lay bold in wait for me
As I awake and conjure for me
Man's perilous life that often ends in dust.

Whisper for me nothingness among the wind.
Sightless truth, you hide from man
The denial of his existence
Until you call him into dust.
Linger on the words I want to say,
Empty me of the words I want to say,
And in the halls of mind nurture,
Haunting my thoughts with images of death.

Choose for me the marks I should wear,
Prepare for me the role I should play.
Hero for the day
Until I return to you.

Honesty

Death calls me to look upon
Man's most dreaded fear,
Removed from life until a time like this
Within the looking glass of my mind.
My spirit returns within itself.
I'll keep my silence now you have gone,
You had always said.
If you should ever lapse
Into the hereafter,
Shed no tears of sadness.

Shattered moments deny me not.
I sit and hope alone instead.
Shattered moments emerge within
Courage and future out of reach.
Speak for me confused soul,
Like feathers touch stir my grief,
Softly summon me within my mind's current
Of fading thoughts bruised by grief.

Hurriedly you flash amid, as if you're still with me,
Then gather hope like withered leaves
Which mimic man's destiny,
Half diseased like fallen angels.
Days of mortal life are just like these,
Soon to be brought to nought.
And in my dreams I ask myself
Are you the train I left behind?
You leave me now to find my way
Upon the reality of life again.

Untitled

Warmth and smiles exchanged,
Bitterness and angry thoughts
Vanish all tarnished collections
Of the love which used to speak
Only in the language of emotions.
Did laughter and love end?

Season of dry winds,
Tossing and turning my passion,
Rushing into being what ought not to be,
Like shaking from a tree a leaf
Which still needs the soil,
Brings to a halt the uninterrupted.

Feelings crash against resistance.
Feelings of intrusion upon
And unsuspecting mind, in a moment
Of affection and tranquillity,
Surrendering all alien thoughts
Intended to shield me, I choose
To ignore,
Alarm bells warn me of nothing,
And gently, so gently, the shadows
Of night fall over my love.

Untitled

Forties, time to reflect,
I cheat on my memories
When I put you aside,
Then like a part I have to play,
You return to return your prop.

Remember when:
Gymslips, ankle-socks, berets,
Pleated skirts, hitched at the waist once outside the door,
Grey shorts, knee-socks, caps,
Boys on one side girls on the other,
Slick hair, beehive, lots of lacquer,

Gobstoppers, lemon sherbets, jamboree bags,
Liquorice all sorts, frozen lollies,
Regular visits in the dentist chair,
Bumps in the playground,
Fights in the toilets.

Yes, I try to put you aside
Now I'm forty.
Every now and then you remind me
Of the memories of my youth.

Sorrow

Console me not in my brokeness.
Patience will not wait for me,
Not in my heart-rending grief.
Tears dilute the injury within me,
I am brought to feebleness.
No strength for tomorrow, today
Does not release me.

And like a haunting, I visit you there.
Timeless time upon time again.
I search for the final curtain
to raise again.
Rehearsal of life after death,
Recite for me the scene of your life
When death was out of reach.

Life, how you feign the reality of death
Only to be fooled by fate.
Death was hid from me as a child,
Revealing that nature was immortal.
Today I search for your life,
It is my birthright not to have been.
I'll not be condoned.

Phantom vessel upon the land of mortals,
Dry sands, barren wells you quench my thirst.
Destiny robs me of reality.
Patience will not wait for me.
Of how I choose to grieve today
Souvenirs in a grief torn handkerchief
Console me not.

The Cloak

Colourless death which preys on man,
Take your dark wings from pale brow.
Bring with you secrets of eternity
When you return to your destiny.
I feel like death itself.

I mourn like a lamenter,
I recount my own life on earth.
I long to go to far away places,
I long to be certain of life's finality
If dust and earth is all I am,

I seek permanence as a treaty
To such a troubled life on earth,
Even if in another world.
Should man come to nothing
Like a decayed leaf that winters,
Only to be trodden on by the rest of nature?
I seek justice for my life as a treaty
For having been born on borrowed time.

If death is to be likened to sleep
Then I have died a million deaths.
In life I have truly died.
If there is an afterlife in death
Then I have lived a million lives.
In death I have truly lived.

I have been host to two enemies,
Death and life, both parasites
Dwelling side by side within my being.
Upon the platform of breath, of breath and breath alone,
Breathe the audience witnessing each act
Until there are no more scenes to be played.

Marriage and Death

Immaculate ivory lies before
This crowded church,
Void of sunshine and radiant smiles.
Among the floral tributes
Her forget-me-nots deck her cushion.
All in black they see none but black.
Now immaculate ivory lies before
This crowded church.

All in black they see none but black,
And from front to back they see black.
Ivory is black before colourless death,
Void of carnations and white roses.
Ivory now beckons me to the graveyard.
Now immaculate ivory lies within
This crowded church.

All in black they lead ivory,
Colourless thoughts of dirges
And rituals in mind's eye so near.
Two weddings and a christening ago
Ivory was black side by side with black.
Now immaculate ivory lies alone before
This crowded church.

Hope

I really do not think
That the Almighty wanted
That I should see you on the brink
Of death's door so sick and pale.
So close your eyes and count to three,
The life hereafter is meant to be.
It's not right for you to see
The earth that covers your loved one here,
Or those who pass from life to death
Would want you to take stock.
So feel the purpose of Christ,
The reason He came to die for us.

For though it is hard to comprehend
That those who live must die on earth,
Fight the choking tears of grief
Which blind you to the truth.
'Tis a sure thing which Christ has said
That all who die in Him will rise again.

So when death comes as a thief
To steal and sting and grieve,
Causing emptiness, sorrow and woe,
Find strength and courage, friend.
We live the evil of time borrowed.
Be strong and firm, for just as seasons come
And seasons go,
So it is death's evil wings,
Wings which clutch and sting,
And when they're here life will cease.
In a moment breath is gone,
Then lies the person who once was,
Still, small nothing, so alien, so different,
No longer part of this life,
But now moved from darkness to light.
For Jesus lives, He is alive and I believe
Waiting for you on the other side.

Untitled

Eternal waves, echoing secrets of the universe
Upon the lapping rocks,
Which visit the shore,
In spasms you twist and turn,
Returning to the stillness within yourself.
Silently you greet me within the shell,
The whispers of nature calling man to listen.

Eternal waves, echoing secrets of the universe
Upon the lapping rocks,
Which visit the shore,
Along the sands that glitter
You visit many a journey to recount,
Taking with you what you witness.

Eternal waves, echoing secrets of the universe
Upon the lapping rocks,
Which visits the shore,
You raise the mountains of the sea,
You disperse your weakness along man's feet,
Calling him to witness your wonder.

Eternal waves, echoing secrets of the universe
Upon the lapping rocks,
Which visit the shore,
Rising to the depths of the sea
As you beat against your shadows,
Take me within your folds.

Eternal waves you deafen me with your roar,
You falsify the taste of my tears,
You delude me with your showers,
You push me by your force,
Eternal waves, splendour of the universe!

Familiar Death

There was a house I used to know.
Not so long ago I do recall
That laughter and cheer lived within its walls
But like a shadow which distorts its shape
The curtains hang without much strength,
The door seems to nod you past.
Life doesn't live here any more.
It seems to be telling its tale.

Take a look around this empty street.
Nature seems half asleep in its witnessing
That the reality of life is to be born with death.
So the laughter and cheer that once was here
Is within every house you look into,
And one day one house will see death,
And its curtains will hang loosely,
Its door will nod you past
And tell you that life died today,
And it will tell you its tale.

Of the many times it witnessed death
In uniform it's been told.
To a hearse it's been a host,
To tears and anger it's stood and watched,
It's seen generations come and go.
In that living room when they had him laid
Among the things he loved very much,
Now seem all meaningless without a word.

So in my grief I asked in vain.
Someone, somewhere had taken this life.
He had so much to give, and loved so much.
And as my anger and rage return.
In my tears and sorrow, I'll search for you
Death does not give in its secret,
Only that as long as life is born with death
It is appointed that man must die.
One day someone's curtain will hang loose,
Then familiar death will be mourned in grief.

Thoughts of Death

Sleep forbids reason upon the mind,
And one day as in death's sleep
Your reason forsakes your mind.
No words from you I'll hear
When in death I demand your breath.
No words from you I'll hear
When I call you to wake for work.
No words from you I'll hear
And hastily you make me grieve.

Flashbacks return to seize
An emptiness already felt inside.
Cruel death takes its vengeance
And tonight you'll not lie with me.
Tonight you'll be alone
Among the company of the hereafter.
Tonight to life you'll not return,
Fooled by sleep you'll never wake.
Tonight restless night and tears.

And tomorrow you'll not return,
To earth you'll not return.
Tomorrow you'll not lie with me,
Tomorrow you'll be alone
Among the company of the hereafter.
Tomorrow to life you'll not return,
Fooled by sleep you'll never wake.
Tomorrow restless night and tears.

Journeys

Visions of the night travelling in the mind
Like the running winds against the rocks,
Like the battling of the sea waves,
Whispering the secrets of the universe.
You return to the nothingness of yourself.

If I could take you into time,
Store you upon the yesterdays and tomorrows
Of my destiny in this uncertain world,
I would ride along with you
And take your wisdom of old.
Yes, in my life you would have purpose.

You are the recreation in each mind
Of that which secrets cannot reveal.
Except in sleep but cannot be accounted for.
Only in sleep will you bring consolation,
Only in sleep will you bring a warning,
Only in sleep will you hold your trial,
Only in sleep will you speak,
Only in sleep will you bring hope,
Only in sleep will you be make believe,

Immortal dream that makes its visitation
Upon mortal man's mind,
Where do you go when man awakens?
Where do you find your strength to reappear,
And when man in his final breath departs
Do you linger on in the minds of his kin?

Vacuousness

Death has made me barren,
I feel I'm a barren fruit.
My navel is buried within me.
The core of my existence is removed.
Into nothingness is the reeling of void,
Emptiness, ashes into nothingness,
Dust into emptiness,
Scattered on to the earth into nothingness.

Death has made me homeless,
Without purpose I move nowhere,
Like a nomad without a resting place,
Like a woman without her breast.
My drinking well is dried up.
The core of my comfort is removed.
Into chaos is the feeling of confusion,
Thundering, clashing into turmoil,
Emptiness, breath into nothingness,
Silence to stillness.
I move house without a choice.

Death has made me afraid,
Like a bat that cannot face light.
I sit all day in my darkened room
Rehearsing how life continues
For those lucky not to be me.
The streets, are they empty
Like how I'm feeling today?
Is life the same as it was last night
When that dreaded message came?
How can it be the same for them
If today I feel as I do?

I look across at your favourite chair,
The slippers that stand along the hall,
The pipe that was never smoked.
And in my grief I look for you.
You will be back tonight won't you?
Don't let me sit up for you again
Until they say dust to dust,
Until they lead you to green pastures,
Until they lay you down to rest,
Until the earth refuses to take you in.
In barrenness I will not be consoled.

Enmity

Death will not speak to me
So I lament in my sorrow.
Enemy of every living being
Speak 'cos I grieve, I moan
Like the waves of the rough sea.
My thoughts return to thoughts within.
What is the secret of your eternity?

Life is no challenge to your duel
'Cos in every race you never lose.
Like a dagger you come to pierce,
Like the wounds which never heal
You destroy and never build.
You are the enemy from within,
In every mortal being you make your home.

Clouds cannot hide your face,
Nor the skies and the earth hide your name.
You are the stranger knocking at each door.
Each silent hour you take your toll.
So be my friend and tell me when
The end is near for me and then
Farewell if that is to be
My destiny. I shall return in peace.

But you do not speak nor do you feel.
You are the silent restlessness
In the minds of mortals.
At the moments of time
When seasons come and seasons go
And as news comes that death is here
I will be asking you once again
To speak to me at last, O death!

Lament

Like a Judas in betrayal
Death would not return his life,
As a ransom for my tears
It would not return his life.

It pierced my side
And tore my bowels apart.
In my bosom I yearn for life
But in my mind I ask for death,
And in my spirit I lament.
In the stillness of my disordered
Life I seek equity.

Bleakness, pangs, solitude, hostility,
This is not the life I knew.
Stranger, alien, detachment, fallacy,
You greet me with cold embrace.
High in the sky I see your existence.
Take me with you on your final ship
Upon the sea that visits the shore.
Bring with it a wave of chaos.

I fear the empty nights,
I fear the silent walls
Which do not echo your voice.
Can life be compared to breath
And breath alone?
You make a fool of man by returning
Dust, ashes, earth, wind, fire,
Eternal death wake for me.

Today

Just for today and only today
I want my life to begin again.
I want to do all the things I've never done,
Go to all the places I've never been,
Say all the things I've never said,
For today life has died and death is born.

Today is gone never to return.
Only in the word will I see it again.
Just like life and just like death,
It is as illusive as a moth
Yet as clear as dawn to dusk.
It is as subtle as a shadow,
Try to chase it and it's gone.

So, tomorrow, I shall say
If I can't have today once more.
And for now at least I'll say
I want my life to start again.
I want today to be everyday,
Say all the things I've never said,
Go to all the places I've never been,
See all the things I've never seen.
In today life and death are side by side.

Thoughts

Chasing thoughts too far from me
Wither, my mind's empty view.
Full of glimpses of what might have been,
Never-ending memories I've seen,
As if it could have been
And wasn't to be.
Thoughts assorted and placed in line,
Select for me to choose,
Shift along from theme to theme
Like a grasshopper in its giant leap.

Rituals

Life is the long ritual,
From the day of breath,
It is the lifting of the curtain,
To the night of stillness.
Life surrounds 'musts' and 'wills'
Every moving act is a scene
Rehearsed before.
Every scene is life
Re-played before
A different audience, in a different place
But it's all the same actors.

An Ode to the Akans

Their colours were red and purple and black.
Tomorrow at sunset it will be white,
And perhaps a little hint of black.
In their grief they cursed death.
They looked to death to explain life,
Their aphorisms the only source of comfort
That death could sting so much.
So the libation is poured again.
They speak to the mortal,
Peace and rest deny him not.
Now his life is called upon,
Now in his death his life is ceased.

In their dozens and singles they came,
Shaking their heads and stretching their hands,
Going from row to row like a ritual.
Each one to his clan greetings
In rhyme to the dirge wails.
The drums began to speak,
The mourners began to weep.
High in the air they are lifted
Upon their shoulders their burden is eased.
They sway and chant to the drum's beating.
Like a climax to the building emotions
The dancers began to shuffle their feet.

See the royal antelope,
It leaps and runs along a crooked path.
Now you see it and then it's gone.
So it is in life with this mimicking.
Try to chase it and it's gone.
And like a hostile enemy
All observation is made from without.
In cunningness it escapes in a flash,
Making a mockery of emotions.
The drums speak its movement
In subtleness it as silent as a lamb.

Their hands beckoning, their feet saying
This is how it was, this was his life.
He had toiled and toiled in vain,
In a land that was not his own.
Never to return to life on earth
But to the ancestors who await.
Patiently they wait to receive
The spirit of this lonely man.
Life and death, marriage and birth,
His custom never died.

Life is a Lonely Road Lived in the Mind

And if I could journey your mind
I would take your lonely road's account,
Because in your life I will ask
Where are those unspoken words you utter?
Life is a lonely road
Lived in the mind.
To try to live it otherwise
Would be a journey without end.
So take me to that place of thoughts,
That place of peace and tranquillity.
And let me live my lonely journey
Within this mind full of thoughts;
A thought of loneliness,
A thought of narrow bends,
A thought of journeys which end in dust.

Untitled

Searching for hours on end
Bringing purpose to naught,
Searching from corner to corner
In a mind full of questions.
Like huge waves
On troubled seas,
Only now and again I guess
I feel the breeze it brought.

Answers to questions not raised
Find solution in a troubled heart,
Taking into the future
What has never been asked at all.
Pillars of strength in a dark hour
Momentary delusions are, truth itself,
Stamping bold prints along its path
Never ending what has begun.

The Cortège

Travelling in slow haste
Along familiar roads,
Time and time again
On a very ordinary day,
Even in disguise as always
It reveals itself today.
Always and never they trail,
Friendly and friendless,
Loved and loveless,
Alone and apart,
Pursued but not chased,
Strange but common,
Solemn but indifferent,
Calm but troubled,
Amazement but not shocking,
We follow, once again,
In footsteps since creation
Till we breathe our last.

Wishes

Wishes deny me all I desire.
Wishful thoughts is all I aspire.
Sounds of leaves beating breeze,
Remindful of how wishes appear.
Sounds of leaves beating twigs
Are all thoughts in a wishful mind.
Suddenly wishes begin to debate.
Wishes debate side by side,
If only to be or not to be.
Wishes of only if, only if.
Wishes repeat scene by scene.
Wishes of dream and reality,
And like a flicker of hope
Moments, precious thoughts, fade,
Purpose or not held as tokens.

My Cat
In memory of Mojo

Gently waiting for me again.
I'll think of warmth as you
Brush me by,
Circling around my legs and feet.
That all familiar ritual,
Day by day by day,
In all man's land without speech.

Your silent voice only you know,
Your tongue forbidden.
You understand I know.
If only I could speak for you
Then you would know you're dear to me.
Friend, joyful, humble companion,
Keep well and I'll be happy for you.

Loss

I die each day a single death,
I keep vigil night after night.
Full of grief it hurts inside.
Envious of the mothered
I want to fight.

Gone for ever out of my sight
I feel what I feel, I feel
Long walks, empty streets,
Desertion is all that's real,
Choked tears, blocked by pain.
I feel what I feel, I feel.

Warmth denies my very existence
Robbed at an untimely hour.
Death and dying living on,
Reassurance not to be found.
I feel what I feel, I feel.

Who am I? I ask myself.
Life's looking glass tells me to search.
In my frame I see a life,
The image of death alive in me.
Barren thoughts of life in death,
I feel what I feel, I feel.

Daydream

Day's and night's timeless hour,
Waiting for love soon to return.
Pounding heartbeats within my breasts
Like marching footsteps along a path,
Waiting to unlock all that's in store,
Call to mind warm caresses,
Tender arms caress me still.

Romance and sweet passion
Just us two.
Whispers of sweet, sweet love
Upon an empty world,
Tender kisses, heart and soul
Bond me still, my senses do yield.

Woo me in the midnight hour
Gracefully surrendering yesterday,
Breaking dawn with ecstasy
At the crossroads of my love.
Bliss I choose in haste.
Forbid my mind the unforsaken.
Surrender in haste my existence.

Lost Love

Still your memories linger on,
Nights of emptiness upon my heart,
Daydreams of the eternal flame
Of love witnessed so many times.
But now hope runs from me
Like a fleeing deserter.
Even my emotions fail me now.
Loss is all I see, and love departed.
Love removed from the seat of purpose,
Meaningful love far from reach.

Love departed brings a halt
To a new beginning in my life.
Like a trembling leaf beaten by rain
A shelter I find so alien now,
Nowhere to lay my troubled heart.
No words from you I'll hear again,
Wet tears on eyes heavy with grief.
Love hurts the ones it should heal,
Loneliness replaces togetherness.

And delusion mocks me still
And hope departs from me,
Like a deserter it flees from me.
When loneliness is all I feel,
Lost love returns to haunt me.
On my forgotten past it haunts me still,
Calling to repent all these years.

Insomnia

Counting sheep always ends.
Tangled sheets, creased pillows
Offer me no sleep tonight at all.
Moving thoughts in mind's turmoil.
Seconds and minutes repeat themselves.
Forty nights refuse me none,
Forty sleeps deny me none.
Remove from eyes temporal death.

Visions in calm deny me none.
Recollection again of midnight hour
Grooves within the mattress weight.
Warmth in armchairs left for sleep,
Slippers dispersed in restlessness,
Halt drunk nightcap thick to the brim,
Counting sheep always ends.